CW01262284

BUSY LITTLE COOK

Judy Bastyra ■ Illustrated by Nicola Smee

CONRAN OCTOPUS

This book belongs to

Contents

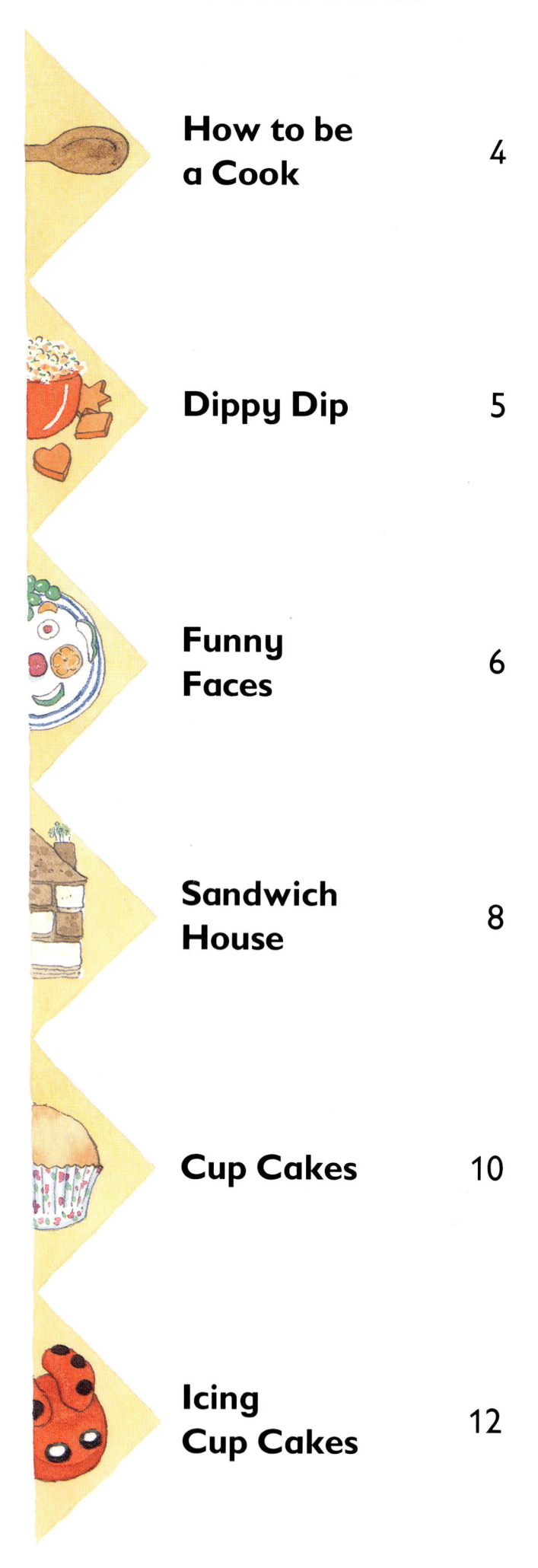

How to be a Cook	4
Dippy Dip	5
Funny Faces	6
Sandwich House	8
Cup Cakes	10
Icing Cup Cakes	12

Design: Alison Fenton
Design assistants: Karen Fenton and Caroline Johnson
Spine illustration: Alison Barclay
Editor: Sue Hook
Photography: Mike Galletly
For her help in preparing food for photography: Sue Sinnott

First published in 1990 by
Conran Octopus Limited
37 Shelton Street, London WC2H 9HN

Reprinted in 1993

© text 1990 Conran Octopus Limited
© illustration 1990 Nicola Smee

All rights reserved.
No part of this book may be reproduced, stored in a retrieval system or transmitted in any form or by any means, electronic, electrostatic, magnetic tape, mechanical, photocopying, recording or otherwise without the prior permission in writing of the publisher.

ISBN 1 85029 258 2

Typeset by Creative Text Limited.
Printed and bound in Singapore

Magic Meringues	14
Mini Pizzas	16
Spice Bunnies	18
Fruit Ices	20
Sparkly Drinks	22
Happy Hot Dog	24
Ice-box Cake	26
Spicy Chicken Parcels	28
Stripy Ice Cream Sundae	30
Party Time!	32

How to be a Cook

Think of the lovely smells which come from the kitchen at mealtimes. Think how delicious your favourite food is. Cooking your own food is great fun.

You will discover lots of exciting new smells and tastes, and you will be very proud when you can say 'I made it myself!'

Find out how you can be a cook

Read all the instructions before you start a recipe. Follow each step carefully and ask an adult to help you whenever you see this sign ★.

Good cooks always get everything ready before they begin. That way they work faster and eat sooner!

Good cooks are clean and tidy cooks. Before you start to cook always wash your hands. Wear an apron. When you finish cooking wash up all your equipment and put everything away.

Are you ready to be a cook?

Dippy Dip

This dip tastes just as good as it looks. Cut a carrot into pretty shapes to dip in.

You will need

1 large tomato

4 tablespoons cream cheese

½ cucumber

1 carrot, washed and peeled

1 teaspoon chopped chives

salt and pepper

Equipment

round-bladed knife

spoon

small mixing bowl

chopping board

small biscuit cutters

Don't break the tomato skin!

1 Cut the top off the tomato and keep it as a lid. Scoop out the inside of the tomato with a spoon.

Let me put the salt and pepper in.

Not too much!

2 Put the cream cheese in your bowl. Chop up the inside of the tomato and the cucumber into small pieces then mix them into the cream cheese. Add the chives, salt and pepper.

Can I dip now?

3 Spoon the mixture into the tomato. Carefully cut the carrot into 5cm lengths. Cut the lengths into thin slices. Cut different shapes with the cutters.

Funny Faces

Try making funny faces from fruit or vegetables. Cut up different kinds with your friends – slices and segments, lots of shapes. See who can make the funniest face.

You will need
Fruit, such as apples, oranges, lemons, pears, grapes, bananas, vegetables, such as tomatoes, carrots, cress, celery, mushrooms, cauliflower.

Equipment

- round-bladed knife
- chopping board
- serving plate

"You wash, I'll dry."

1 Wash the fruit and vegetables you want to use, before cutting them up.

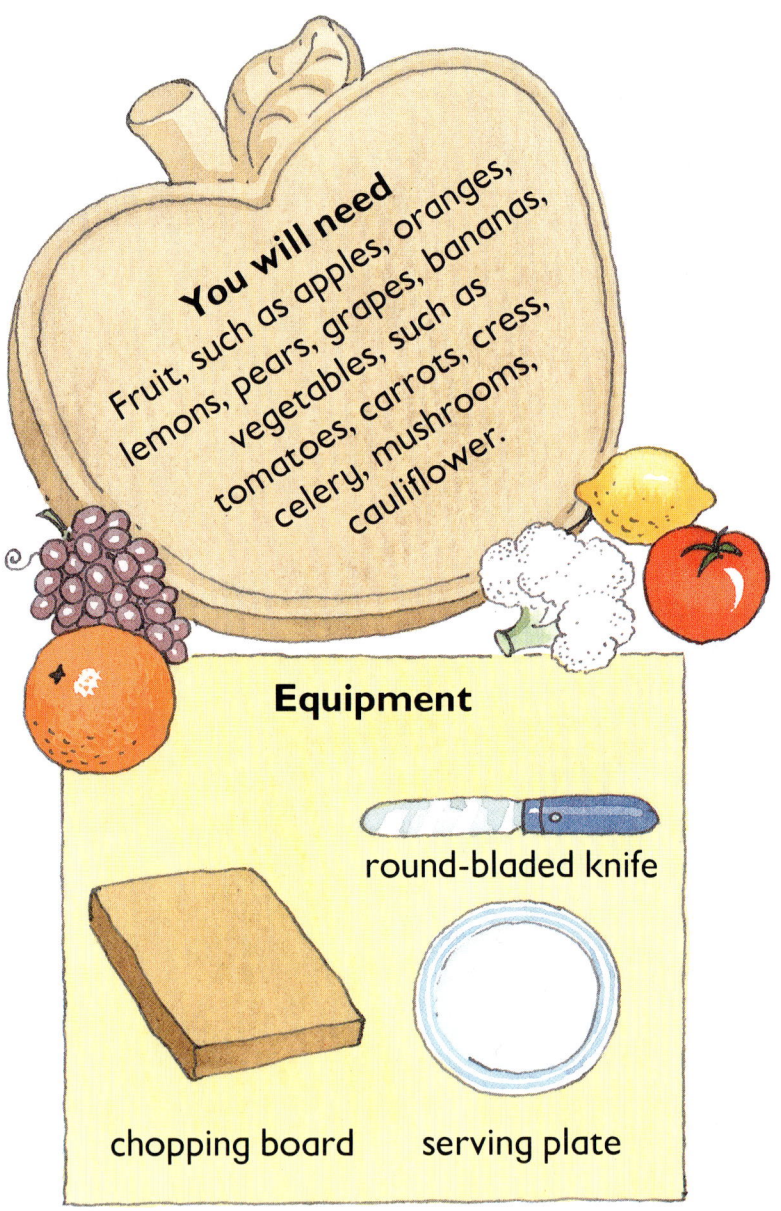

"Are you going to use all vegetables?"

"A squeeze of lemon juice will stop bananas and apples going brown."

"A slice of apple makes a good smile."

"My face is going to have rosy tomato cheeks."

2 Prepare the fruit and vegetables, peeling if necessary. Cut very carefully into slices or separate into segments.

3 Choose the segments and slices you want to make your face.

"Leave room for the eyes."

"I'm using cress for hair."

4 When the faces are finished, they can be served with yoghurt for fruit faces or mayonnaise for vegetables.

How to cut slices

1. Always hold a knife by its handle. Make sure the cutting edge is facing down.

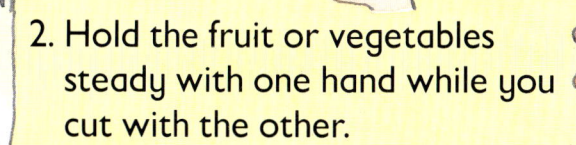

2. Hold the fruit or vegetables steady with one hand while you cut with the other.

3. Mind your fingers – check they are not near the blade of the knife.

Sandwich House

Make some sandwiches with your favourite fillings. Cut them into different shapes and build a house for tea.

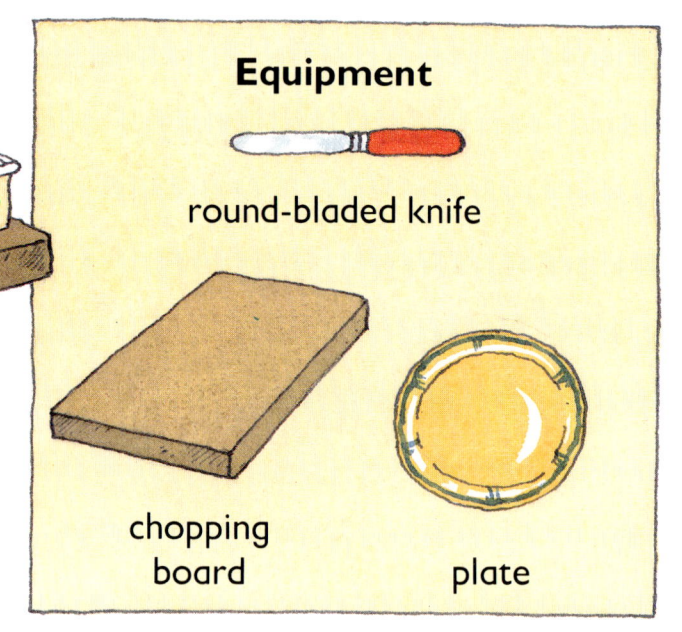

You will need

6 slices brown bread
4 slices white bread
soft margarine
sandwich filling

Equipment

round-bladed knife

chopping board

plate

How to spread

When you are spreading, don't press too hard or the bread will break.

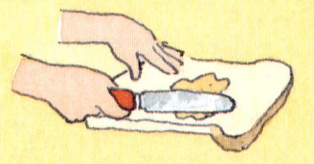

How to cut off crusts

Hold the bread steady with one hand and cut away the crusts along one side with the other hand.

Turn the bread around as you cut the crust off each side. Mind your fingers.

Choose your favourite filling – cucumber, tomato, cheese, lettuce, banana, peanut butter. Make 3 brown sandwiches and 2 white sandwiches, spreading the margarine and filling carefully. Cut the crusts off the sandwiches.

You cut, I'll build them up.

1 Cut one sandwich into 3 and put the strips on top of each other.

I'd like another one for the chimney.

Make sure they fit on the base.

2 Cut a white sandwich and a brown sandwich into 9 squares each.

Can I eat the extra sandwich?

3 Finally put the roof on – cut 2 more sandwiches in half to make 3 triangles to fit the top of the house.

Cup Cakes

Cup cakes are so easy to make. Weigh two eggs and use the same weight of flour, margarine and sugar. Mix them together then put the mixture in pretty paper cases. They will cook very quickly.

Equipment

- scales
- wooden spoon
- teaspoon
- paper cases
- small bowl
- mixing bowl
- patty tins

You will need

- 2 eggs
- caster sugar
- soft margarine
- self-raising flour
- ★ adult help

Get everything you need ready before you begin. The oven should be switched on to 180C/350F/Gas 4.

Makes about 16.

1 Weigh your eggs. If the two eggs weigh 100 grams (4oz) you will need the same weight each of margarine, sugar and flour.

How to crack an egg

1. Tap the egg on the side of a bowl so that a crack appears on the shell.

2. Put your thumbs on either side of the crack and gently pull the shell apart so the egg slides out into the bowl.

2 Cream the margarine and sugar together in the bowl until it is light and fluffy.

4 Put a spoonful of mixture into each case.
★ Cook the cakes in the oven for about 15 minutes.

3 Add the eggs to the mixture with the flour, a little of each at a time. Mix well.

5 When the cakes are cooked, leave them to cool on a wire rack.

Icing Cup Cakes

Have some fun with your cup cakes. With coloured icing and sweets you can turn them into funny animals.

You will need

lots of cup cakes (see page 10)

100g (4oz) soft margarine or butter

250g (8oz) icing sugar

a variety of food colouring

assorted sweets

Equipment

scales

mixing bowl

wooden spoon

mug

round-bladed knife

sieve

metal spoons

several small bowls

Making the butter icing

Can you have a go now?

1. Put the margarine or butter in a very large mixing bowl. Sieve the icing sugar, a little at a time, mixing all the time. Continue beating the mixture until it is smooth and has no lumps.

The green is wonderful.

2. Divide the mixture up into several small bowls then add a few drops of food colouring to each bowl. Mix in each colour with a metal spoon.

Hints and tips for icing

1. Use metal spoons to mix in the colour, as wooden spoons will stain.

2. Brush off all the crumbs from the cakes before you start to ice.

3. Fill a mug full of warm water and dip a knife into it to help smooth out the icing.

The dragon
Cut 4 cup cakes across, making smaller slices each time. Cover in green icing and position on a plate. Make scales from chocolate wafer mints. Cut slots for the scales. Make a tongue from liquorice and eyes and feet from orange and other coloured smarties.

The mouse
Cut 1 cup cake in half. Trim one end to make a nose. Cover with pink icing. Use smarties for the eyes and slice a marshmallow for the ears. Liquorice makes a tail and spaghetti the whiskers.

The frog
Cut a cup cake across the centre, but do not cut completely through, to make a mouth. Cover in green icing, add two sweets for eyes, two for the legs and another for the mouth.

The ladybird
Cut off the top of the cup cake and then cut the top in two to make the two wings. Cover the cake and the wings in red icing. Put the wings in place. Decorate with small pieces of liquorice and use smarties for the eyes.

The pig
Cover the top of a cup cake with pink icing. Use scissors to cut a marshmallow into a small circle for the nose. Cut triangle sweets for ears. Add dolly mixture eyes and a red liquorice tail.

Magic Meringues

These pretty meringues taste as good as they look. Make some as presents or for a birthday party tea.

You will need

3 eggs
pinch of salt
150g (6oz) caster sugar
edible coloured cake balls
food colouring (if you like)
★ adult help

Get everything ready before you begin. Take out the eggs from the fridge, line the trays with paper and make sure the bowl is clean and dry. ★Set the oven to low, 75C/150F/Gas 1/2.
Makes about 36.

Equipment

saucer
cup
big bowl
small bowl
scales
electric beater/rotary whisk
teaspoon
baking tray
silicone paper

1. Crack the eggs and separate the whites from the yolks. Put the whites in the large mixing bowl, add a pinch of salt and a few drops of food colouring if using. ★Whisk until whites are light and fluffy.

2. ★ Add the sugar slowly to the egg whites, beating slowly all the time. Continue beating until the mixture is thick and shiny.

3. Drop teaspoons of the mixture on to the baking tray, spaced well apart.

4. Sprinkle over the coloured balls. ★Cook in the oven for 2 hours. ★Turn off the heat and leave to cool in the oven for a while.

Speech bubbles:
- "You can tell if they are whisked enough if you turn the bowl over and the mixture doesn't fall out."
- "Can I use brown sugar?"
- "Yes but the meringues will be golden brown instead of white."
- "Use another teaspoon to push the mixture off the spoon."
- "Can I lick the bowl?"
- "Why were they left in the oven?"
- "It helps them to dry out and then they are even more crunchy."

How to separate an egg

1. Crack the egg gently into a saucer.

2. Cover the yolk with a cup.

3. Gently tip the white into the large mixing bowl, holding the yolk in place with the cup.

Mini Pizzas

Pizzas smell so good as they cook. Make some funny face mini pizzas to share with your friends.

Equipment

- round-bladed knife
- rolling pin
- mixing bowl
- wooden spoon
- jug
- baking tray
- pastry brush
- glass or biscuit cutter

You will need
145g (5½oz) packet pizza dough mix
flour
oil
2 tablespoons tomato ketchup or purée
4 tomatoes, sliced
green and red peppers, seeded and sliced
100g (4oz) grated Cheddar cheese
dried oregano or mixed herbs
stoned black olives
salt and pepper
★ adult help

Weigh all the ingredients before you begin. ★ The oven should be switched on to 220C/425F/Gas 7, after you have made the dough. Oil the baking trays. **Makes 6 pizzas.**

My dough's getting thicker.

1 Empty the packet of pizza mix into a bowl and add 200ml (7fl.oz) of hand-hot water. Mix to a dough.

Is this how you knead it?

Yes, push it away with one hand and pull it back with the other one.

Let's sprinkle cheese to make hair.

Look at my green pepper mouth.

2 When it is all mixed in, take the dough out of the bowl, shape into a ball and knead for about 10 minutes until it is stretchy and shiny.

4 Brush the pizzas with oil and spread with ketchup or purée. Sprinkle over the herbs, salt and pepper. Make funny faces with the tomatoes, peppers, cheese and olives. ★Cook for 12-15 minutes.

I'll use up the dough

We can roll these bits too.

Fast Pizzas

If you are in a hurry, you can use crumpets or muffins as the base for the mini pizzas instead of the dough mix.

3 ★Turn on the oven. Sprinkle a little flour onto your work surface and roll out the dough. Use a glass or biscuit cutter to cut out circles and put them on the baking tray.

17

Spice Bunnies

Make some little bunnies sitting on grass.
★ Turn on the oven to 180C/350F/Gas 4.
Makes about 12 bunnies and 4 bases.

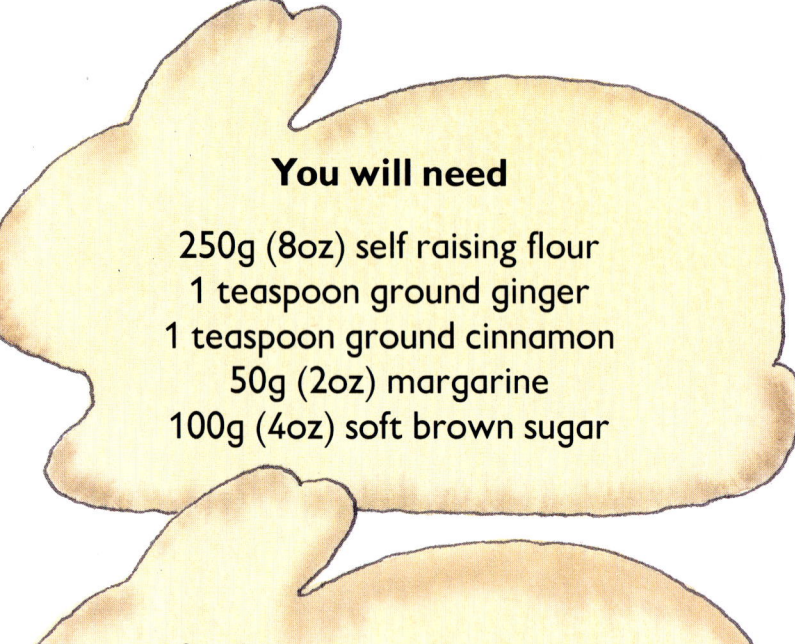

You will need

250g (8oz) self raising flour
1 teaspoon ground ginger
1 teaspoon ground cinnamon
50g (2oz) margarine
100g (4oz) soft brown sugar

2 tablespoons golden syrup
1 egg, beaten
100g (4oz) icing sugar
2 tablespoons desiccated coconut
green food colouring
★ adult help

Equipment

- scales
- small bowl
- round-bladed knife
- tablespoon
- rolling pin
- teaspoon
- bunny biscuit cutters
- mixing bowl
- baking sheets
- sieve
- silicone paper
- fork

1 Sift the flour, ginger and cinnamon into the mixing bowl. Add the margarine and sugar and rub together with your fingers.

I cut the margarine into little bits.
It will look like breadcrumbs when it's mixed.

2 Beat the golden syrup and egg together with a fork, then stir them into the flour mixture and mix until smooth.

I'm going to stir this well.
I'll sprinkle some flour for you.

I'm going to press out some bunnies.

The coconut grass looks real.

These bunnies stick better with some icing sugar on their bottoms.

3 ▸ Sprinkle the flour onto the work surface and rolling pin and roll out the dough evenly. Using the biscuit cutter cut out 12 bunnies. Roll out the rest of the dough. Divide into 4 flat shapes. Line the baking sheets.

5 ▸ Mix the icing sugar with a little water until it is just runny enough to spread. Add a little green colouring to the coconut. Ice the flat bases. Sprinkle over the green coconut then add the bunnies, 3 on each base.

I think it's hard enough now.

Let's take them off carefully.

Rolling out pastry

1. Sprinkle flour onto the work surface and rolling pin.
2. Shape the pastry into a ball. Press it flat with the rolling pin.
3. Roll out evenly. Always push the rolling pin away from you. Press on it gently all the time.

4 ▸ Put the bunnies on one baking sheet and the bases on the other. ★Bake the bunnies for 8 minutes and the bases for 12-15 minutes. ★Take out of the oven. When the dough is cool and hard remove from the baking sheets.

Fruit Ices

Choose your favourite juice, add some pretty fruit slices, freeze them and you have a healthy, licky lolly.

You will need

For 4 lollies

lime cordial or fruit juice

small slices of strawberries, apples, cherries, kiwi and mandarin segments

★ adult help

Equipment

jug

4 lolly moulds

lolly sticks

small tray

Mine looks like a flower.

I'm going to use lime now.

2 Arrange the fruit slices in the moulds and very gently pour in the rest of the juice. Put the moulds back in the freezer until completely frozen.

I'm using lime first.

They're yummy!

1 Push the lolly sticks halfway into the moulds. Place the moulds on a tray and half fill them with cordial or juice. Put the moulds in the freezer for 1 hour, or until frozen.

3 Take the lollies out of the freezer, leave for a few minutes, then carefully take them out of the moulds.

Make flavoured ice cubes

Fill the ice tray with lots of different drinks: blackcurrant cordial, orange juice, lime juice, pineapple juice, milk, chocolate milk and even yoghurt. You can add slices of fruit to make it look prettier.

To make ice lollies, cover with cling film. ★Push wooden cocktail sticks or lolly sticks into their centres. The cling film will hold the sticks upright.

Make a huge yoghurt lolly by freezing a pot of your favourite fruit yoghurt. Before you put it in the freezer, push a lolly stick into the centre, through the foil top.

Sparkly Drinks

Here are two drinks you can make for yourself in a few minutes, Fresh Fizzy Lemonade and Witches' Brew, just right to frighten someone on a dark night!

You will need

For the Lemonade

2 lemons

5 tablespoons sugar

2 cups fizzy water

ice cubes

For the Witches' Brew

120ml (4 fl oz) blackcurrant cordial

fizzy water

4 scoops vanilla ice cream

strawberry syrup

Equipment

grater

tablespoon

mixing jug

round-bladed knife

chopping board

ice cream scoop

lemon squeezer

2 glasses for each drink

To make the Lemonade

"Mind the lemon pips."

"Are you ready yet?"

1 Grate about 1 teaspoon of the lemon zest from one of the lemons and put into the jug. Cut each lemon in half and squeeze out the juice. Pour into the jug.

2 Stir the sugar into the juice. Wait until it has dissolved then add the fizzy water.

To make the Witches' Brew

It's a witchy colour!

1 Divide the blackcurrant cordial between the two glasses. Pour in the fizzy water.

Mine's going to bubble over.

I'm going to use a straw.

2 Add 2 scoops of ice cream to each glass. Squeeze over some strawberry syrup and try to drink it before it bubbles over!

I like the cherries.

3 Add the crushed ice and decorate the side of the glass with a slice of lemon and a cherry.

Happy Hot Dog

This hot dog is great fun to make but he's so friendly it's almost a shame to eat him.

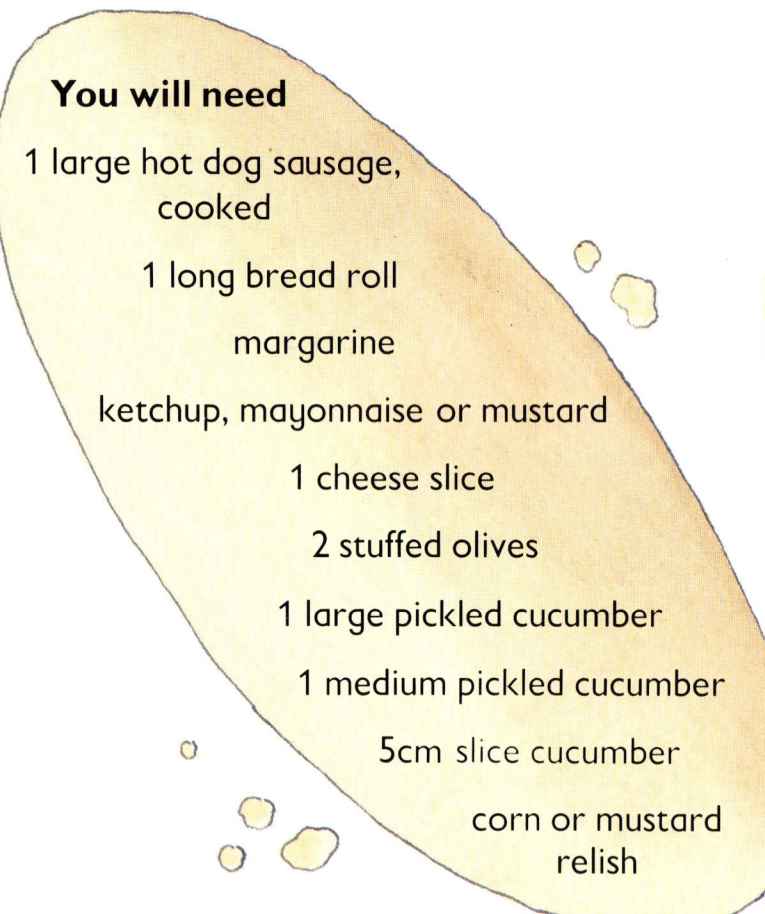

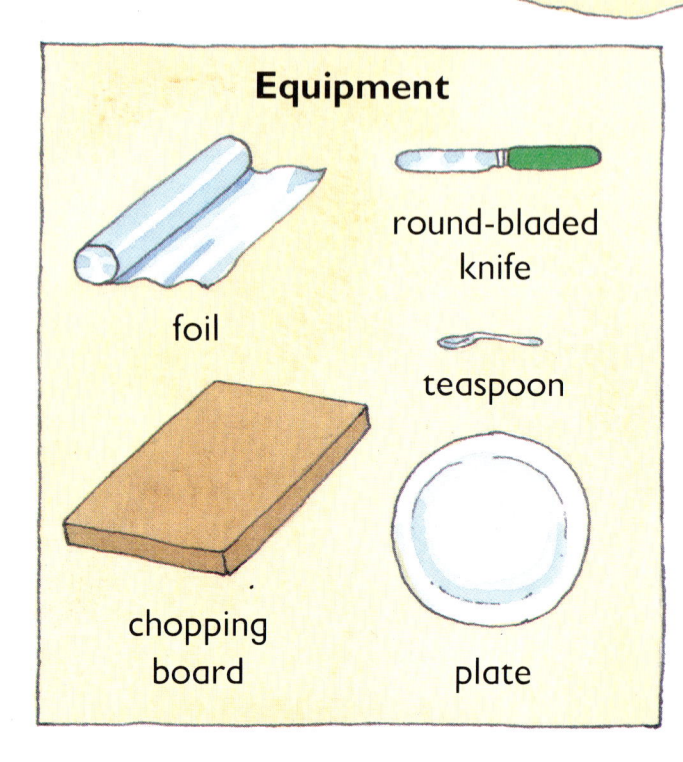

You will need

1 large hot dog sausage, cooked

1 long bread roll

margarine

ketchup, mayonnaise or mustard

1 cheese slice

2 stuffed olives

1 large pickled cucumber

1 medium pickled cucumber

5cm slice cucumber

corn or mustard relish

Equipment

foil

round-bladed knife

teaspoon

chopping board

plate

Get everything ready before you begin. Don't forget to wash your hands. Wrap the sausage in foil to keep it warm.

Make room to put the margarine in.

You have to do this very carefully.

1 Slice the roll about half way along. Push the knife down the middle of the roll, making a hole for the sausage. Spread with margarine.

The sausage has gone all the way in.

There's his nose!

2 Add ketchup, mayonnaise or mustard and put the sausage inside the roll, leaving a little bit showing for a nose.

I'll cut both ears.

So they're the same size. You're clever.

3 Cut the cheese slice in half for ear shapes. Fix the ears in place on each side of the sausage.

4 Cut the large pickled cucumber into 4 pieces and use them as legs. Make a slit at the other end of the roll and push in the smaller pickled cucumber for a tail. Press the olives into the roll for eyes.

5 Make the dog's bowl by scooping out the seeds from the middle of the piece of cucumber. Fill it with relish for his dinner.

Ice-box Cake

Here is a cake that you don't bake! All you do is mix the ingredients together, freeze them and hey presto you have a delicious chocolate cake – just ready to slice and eat.

You will need

75g (3oz) butter
25g (1oz) sugar
4 tablespoons cocoa powder
2 tablespoons single cream
50g (2oz) glacé cherries
12 digestive biscuits

Equipment

- greaseproof paper
- chopping board
- 450g (1lb) loaf tin
- wooden spoon
- mixing bowl
- round-bladed knife
- tablespoon
- rolling pin

Get everything ready and weighed out before you begin. Line the tin with greaseproof paper. Cut the glacé cherries in half. **Makes 12 slices.**

We'll take it in turns to stir.

This will taste yummy.

1 Soften the butter with the back of your wooden spoon then add the sugar and beat together until light and fluffy. Stir in the cream and cocoa powder and mix until it is smooth and creamy.

It's a good way to use up broken biscuits.

We'll do it with lots of different biscuits next time.

2 Put the biscuits between two sheets of greaseproof paper. Crush them with the rolling pin. Leave some quite big pieces as well as crumbs.

"It just comes half-way up the tin."

"I'll smooth the top with a knife before we cover it."

Some more ideas

1. You can use the mixture to make crunchy truffles. Roll it into 12 balls, then roll them in chocolate vermicelli and place on a greased baking sheet. Cover with cling wrap before freezing.

3 Mix the crushed biscuits and cherries into the chocolate mixture and spoon it into the lined tin. Cover with more greaseproof paper and place in the freezer for about 3 hours or until the mixture has set.

"I'm going to cut it into little squares to make it last longer."

"It's thawed enough to eat."

2. For another tasty version of the cake, use muesli and sultanas instead of the biscuits and cherries.

4 Turn the cake onto a plate, remove the greaseproof paper and leave to thaw for 30 minutes. Cut into 12 slices, or small squares.

Spicy Chicken Parcels

Make little parcels and cook your own barbecue supper in the oven. The parcels help to cook the food quickly and seal in all the goodness and flavour.

Get everything ready before you begin.

★ Turn the oven to 400F/200C/Gas 6.

Makes 2 spicy chicken suppers.

You will need

2 tablespoons tomato ketchup

2 teaspoons runny honey

½ teaspoon Worcestershire sauce

2 tablespoons soft butter or margarine

2 teaspoons fresh, chopped herbs or 1 teaspoon dried herbs (chives, sage or parsley)

salt and pepper

2 chicken legs

2 small to medium size potatoes

1 long bread roll

★ adult help

Equipment

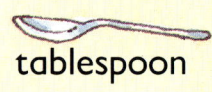

- small mixing bowl
- kitchen paper 
- tablespoon 
- foil
- teaspoon
- fork 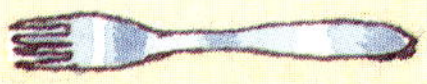
- round-bladed knife 
- baking tray

This smells scrummy!

I bet it tastes scrummy too!

1 Make the barbecue sauce. Mix the tomato ketchup, honey and Worcestershire sauce together with a fork. Add salt and pepper.

Delicious herb bread

1. Put the softened butter or margarine in your clean mixing bowl. Add the dried or fresh herbs and mash together with a fork.

2. Taste the herb butter. Add a sprinkling of salt if you think it is needed.

3. Cut slits in the bread and spread the butter.

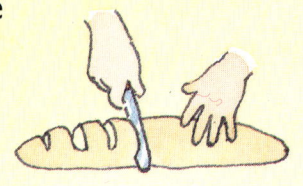

2 Wash and dry the potatoes with kitchen paper and prick them with a fork. ★Wrap them in foil, put them on the baking tray and place in the oven. Cook for 30 minutes.

3 Wash and dry the chicken pieces. Place each one on a piece of foil and spoon over the sauce. Fold the edges of the foil together to make parcels. Wash the mixing bowl.

4 ★Put the parcels on the baking tray with the potatoes. Cook for another 15 minutes. Make your herb bread while you wait. ★Wrap it in foil and cook with the chicken and potatoes for 15 more minutes.

5 ★After 1 hour your supper will be ready. ★If you want crispy chicken and bread, unwrap the foil and cook them for 10 more minutes.

Stripy Ice Cream Sundae

See how colourful you can make these huge ice cream sundaes with your favourite flavoured ice cream, jelly and fruit. This recipe uses red and green jelly but you can choose whichever colours you like best.

You will need

1 packet green jelly

1 packet red jelly

2 bananas

2 satsumas

300ml (10fl.oz) double cream

500ml (16.5fl.oz) Neopolitan ice cream

chocolate vermicelli

4 chocolate flakes

★ adult help

Equipment

2 bowls

measuring jug

ice cream scoop

tablespoon

round-bladed knife

round-ended scissors

1 mixing bowl

whisk

4 tall ice cream glasses

Get everything ready before you begin. **Makes 4.**

1 First of all make the jellies. Follow the instructions on the packets.

"We'll put them in the fridge to set."

"The jelly squelches when you cut it."

"I'll take the pith off the satsumas."

2 When the jellies have set, chop them into small pieces. Peel the bananas and satsumas. Slice the bananas and divide the satsumas into segments.

"Whisk the cream slowly."

"It will turn to butter if I go too fast."

3 ★ Whisk the cream very carefully until it stands in firm peaks. Make sure you don't whisk it too much.

"Leave enough space for lots of cream on top."

"Let's eat these two now."

4 Now you can make your ice cream sundaes. Start with a spoonful of red jelly then add some fruit, then a scoop of ice cream. Continue making layers, using a different coloured jelly and ice cream each time until you get to the top. Keep a few slices of banana and satsuma segments to use for decoration.

5 Finish each sundae by covering the top with the whipped cream and decorating it with chocolate vermicelli, fruit and chocolate flake.

Hot chocolate sauce

Here's how to make chocolate sauce to serve with your sundae or with plain ice cream.

All you need is

100g (4oz) plain chocolate

25g (1oz) butter

2 tablespoons milk

1. Break up the chocolate into squares and put them into a pan with the butter and milk.

2. ★ Put the pan over a very low heat and slowly melt the ingredients. Stir all the time with a wooden spoon. You can eat the sauce hot or cold.

Party Time!

Now you are a cook why not have a party for your friends? Here are some ideas for party food you can make yourself.

▶ Make some tiny square sandwiches, just like your Sandwich House on page 8.

Try these fillings:

Sardines mashed with a few drops of lemon juice

Cream cheese with celery and apple slices

Peanut butter and cranberry jelly

▶ Turn your cup cakes into butterflies. Carefully cut a slice off the top. Cut the slice in half. Spread butter icing on top of the cake and stick the two wings in place.

▶ Put pizza toppings on little slices of French loaf. ★Toast them under the grill. Try ham and pineapple, tuna and sweetcorn or sausage and mushroom, on top of the tomato purée and herbs.

▶ Be sure to add your favourite recipe. Serve with your Sparkly Drinks (page 22) and have fun!

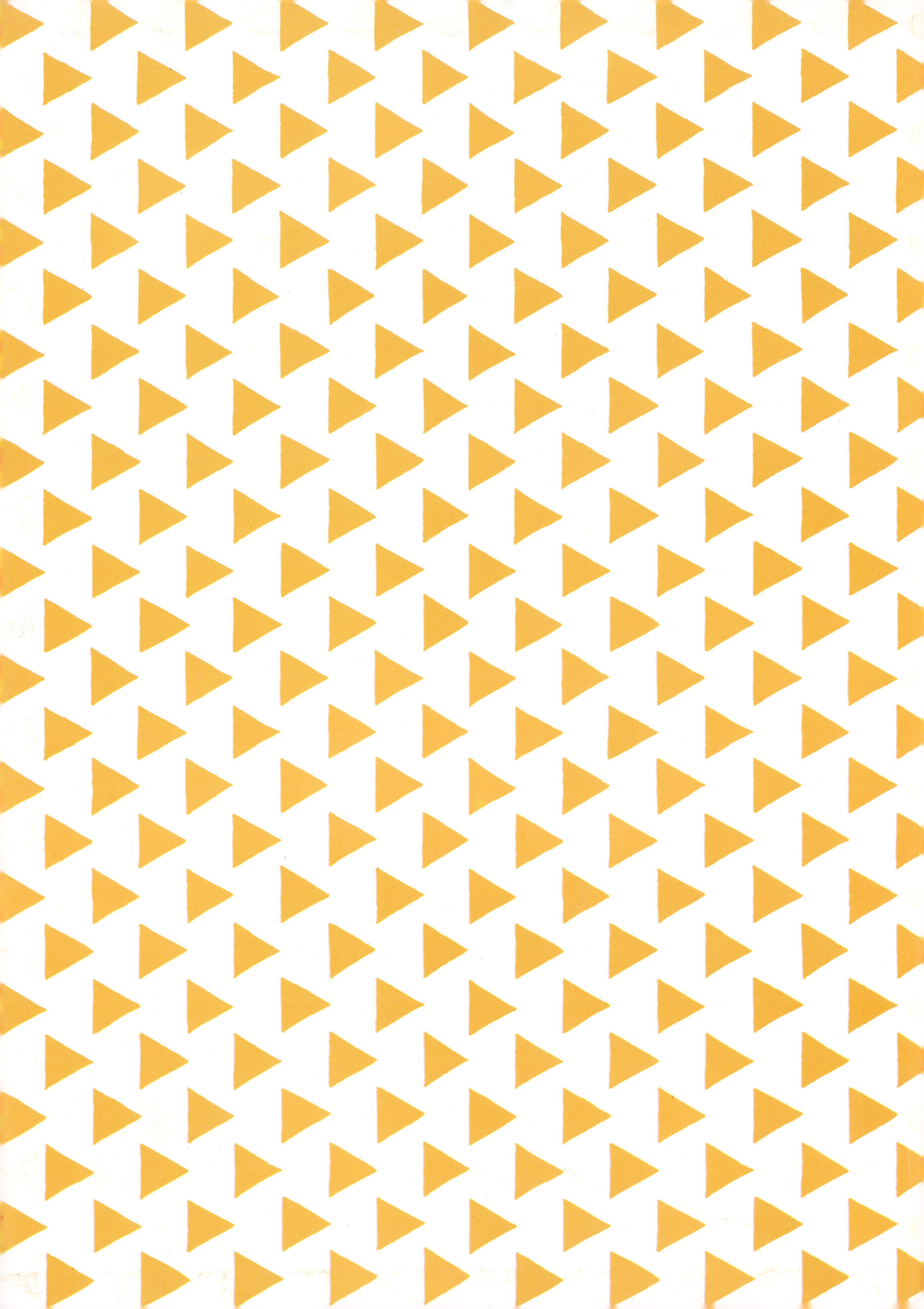